The Golf Rules

~ Etiquette ~

The Golf Rules

~ Etiquette ~

Enhance Your Golf Etiquette by Watching Others' Mistakes

The Story of a Municipal Golfer
on a Country Club Course

Richard E. Todd

Bobconeal Select

Amherst, Ohio

Published by Loconeal Select. Loconeal Select books can be ordered
through booksellers, Handcar Press Distribution or by contacting:
www.loconeal.com 216-772-8380 or www.TheGolfRules.com

For information about custom editions, special sales, and premium
corporate purchases, please visit www.TheGolfRules.com

ISBN: Softcover   978-1-940466-17-0   October 2014
       Ebook (EPUB)978-1-940466-19-4   October 2014

This book was printed in the United States of America.

www.TheGolfRules.com

DEDICATION

To every golfer in the world who plays the game of golf, is in awe of its ancient beginnings, respects the gentlemen's code of conduct, and enjoys the challenge of each round.

To my dad, for providing me years of golfing experiences, which I can draw from for my writing.

To my wife, Christine, for all her love, support, encouragement, and patience while I chased my passion and a little white ball.

To God, for putting the right people in my life and on my path to help me along my writing journey.

INTRODUCTION

YOU DON'T HAVE to be proficient at golf to love it or play the game. However, golf etiquette is a different story.

Proper behavior is quite necessary on the golf course as golf is more than a game, and how we play it is a reflection of its ancient history and who we are and how our morals are perceived. Poor behavior on the course can affect the way you are seen off the course.

People will accept poor scores but never will they forgive poor behavior.

Golf is a gentleman's game, where you are your own referee and conscience. You must enforce the rules and manners by which you play.

Regardless of your skill level, always show good manners on the golf course by following proper etiquette and remember to enjoy the game.

PROLOGUE

"HELLO?"

"Hi. Is this Nicholas?"

"Yes."

"Nicholas, this is Susan with the county community coalition. Congratulations! You won the 'golf for a day' drawing to benefit the local shelter."

"Really? That's great. Thanks."

"Thank you, Nicholas. It's donations from people like you that help our residents. I'll send your award packet and letter in the mail, but the golf course has already been given your name. Just give them a call to confirm you will attend their event. Thanks again, Nicholas. Have fun at the course. Goodbye."

"Bye," Nicholas said as he set down the phone and turned to his wife. "I won, I won, I won!" he shouted.

"What did you win? Who was on the phone?" Hannah asked.

"I won a round of golf to Fox Hunters Country Club. You know, that private and expensive golf course on the edge of town."

"That's great. I know you've always wanted to play there."

"I definitely have. But I'm not a great golfer and I'm not totally sure how to conduct myself at a country club."

"You learned all about the rules of golf from that book

you read last year, The Golf Rules-Stroke Play, and you follow them on Facebook. Don't they have some education on golf etiquette?"

"Why yes, they do have a book on that. Great idea. I'll go get a copy, right after I call the course."

~~~

"Good afternoon. This is Fox Hunters Country Club, Mr. Grey speaking. How I may be of service?"

"Um, hi. This is Nicholas Filler. I was told I won a round of golf there."

"Yes. Congratulations, sir. We have been expecting your phone call. How may I assist you?"

"Well, I was calling to confirm I'll be at the event and to see what other information I may need as I've never played there." [If you are to play at a course you have never visited, it's best to contact them in advance for any local rules, directions, or other necessary information you may need.]

"Yes, very good, sir. Your tee-time is 8:35. [A tee-time is when your group is expected to start play. You should be at the first tee at least fifteen minutes prior to that]. You will be provided with access to our locker room facilities. You may also take advantage of our driving range. There are individuals to collect your golf bag upon your arrival."

"As this is a fund raiser and you are not a member, please feel free, but not obligated, to tip the staff for exemplary services. [The PGA offers this advice as a best practice for tipping. For valet, $1-$2; at a bag drop/bag room, $2-$5; for a locker room attendant, $3-$5 (for shoe cleaning); for cart staff, $2-$5 (for club cleaning), and for staff at a beverage cart, tip 15%-20% of the price of the

RICHARD E. TODD

items.] If for any reason you are unable to attend, we expect you will notify the clubhouse at least a day in advance." [Events can come up that require you to change plans. If you are ever unable to make a tee-time you should call the course as early as possible so they can fill your slot.]

"Additionally, Fox Hunters Country Club does not allow metal spikes on the course [most courses only allow non-metal spiked shoes. This is done for care of the course. Most shoes manufactured today have soft spikes.], no spiked shoes of any kind are allowed in the dining or social hall [you should have a spare pair of shoes available, you never know when you might need them. You don't want to be stuck in a pair of wet, muddy, or uncomfortable shoes all day], and, it goes without saying, proper attire is required at all times. [You may also want to have a spare shirt available for after your round.] Our minimum is a collared shirt and slacks. [Knowing the expectations saves you from arriving and not being allowed on the course, not being able to play, or not being able to enter certain parts of the clubhouse.] Are there any question I haven't answered, sir?"

"No. I think that's everything."

"Very good. If you should need anything else don't hesitate to contact us. We look forward to your arrival. Goodbye."

"Thanks. Bye."

"How'd it go?" asked Hannah.

"Well, I learned a lot, but I also learned there's a lot I don't know. I'm glad I called, but I definitely have to get reading that book."

"Are you excited about today?" asked Hannah.

"Extremely," replied Nicholas. "I have my clubs packed, and I'm mentally prepared. That book was very educational. I'll be leaving soon."

"Really? Why are you leaving so soon?"

"You are supposed to arrive early. There are lots of things to do before you start playing," Nicholas stated. [Always arrive in plenty of time to change shoes or clothes, check in for your tee time, warm up and practice, load your bag on a cart (pull or electric), and arrive at the first tee before your starting time.]

"OK. Have fun," Hannah said as Nicholas walked out the door and headed off to the golf course.

A short drive later, he arrived at the entrance to Fox Hunters Country Club. Nicholas drove under a massive wrought iron arch that stood at the beginning of the road before driving through a winding path, edged with holly bushes and lined on both sides by giant oak trees. Periodically he passed bronze statues of foxes, beagles, and huntsmen in different action poses. Coming to a fork in the road, he stopped and read the signpost. 'Clubhouse' was carved into a wooden arrow pointing to the right, and 'Maintenance' on an arrow pointing to the left. [Courses may have multiple sites that are not geographically close. Watch for directions if you are unfamiliar with the layout.]

As he headed in the direction of the clubhouse he saw another arrow pointing to the right that read 'bag drop'. [Some courses have designated areas where your clubs are to be left before your round. This alleviates the need to carry them from the parking area.] As he followed the sign, a sharply dressed individual wearing an old fashion fox hunter outfit waved his car to a stop just inches from himself, then walked to the car window.

"Good morning sir, welcome to Fox Hunters Country Club. May I have your name?"

"Hi. I'm Nicholas Filler."

"Good morning, Mr. Filler. Would you please release your trunk latch so the lads can gather your clubs and belongings?" [Some bag drops have designated individuals to help unload your equipment.]

Nicholas complied.

"Thank you, sir. If you'll step out of the car one of our lads will park it for you. I see you have a duffle. Shall we put that in your locker with your shoes?" [Different levels of valets may present themselves. Some of these services are only found at more upscale courses. Do what feels right for you.]

"Uh, sure. Thanks".

"No trouble, sir. Your clubs will be set outside the clubhouse. If you just walk through these doors and down the hall, you'll see our pro-shop manager who'll help you from there. Have a good round, sir," he said, holding open large, old, oak doors, covered with carvings of fox hunts, for Nicholas to pass through.

The entire length of the long hallway was covered with glass cases, full of trophies from many different tournaments – community, city, state, and national events; annual club matches, and long standing competitions between other clubs, just to name a few. At the end of the hallway was the pro-shop, filled with merchandise of all types. There were racks of shirts, jackets, and pants, all adorned with the FHCC logo, along with an ample supply of equipment for sale, including golf clubs, balls, gloves, and miscellaneous accessories. [Most courses have some form of merchandise for sale. You may purchase whatever you want or need, either before or after your round.]

There's definitely not this much of a choice at the golf store on Cleveland Street, thought Nicholas.

In the center of the room was a large, round desk. The man in the center caught Nicholas' attention.

"Good morning, sir. How I can help you?" he asked.

"Hi. I'm Nicholas Filler. I'm here for the outing."

"Filler, Filler. Here you are. Thanks for checking in, Mr. Filler. Please, look around. If there's anything you need, let me know. When you are ready, the locker rooms are to your left, the restaurant is on your right, and straight through those doors will take you to the putting area, driving range, and starter's house." [Most courses have either a restaurant, snack bar, or food cart with items for purchase. If you are at a private club as a guest then check with your member host first. Some clubs don't take cash or require all purchases be assigned to a member.]

"Thanks," Nicholas said then scanned the apparel on his way through the room.

An older gentleman, wearing a vest covered in pictures of golfers from the 1800s, welcomed Nicholas as he entered the locker area. "Good morning, sir. My name is Earl. May I have your name?"

"Nicholas Filler."

RICHARD E. TODD

"Thank you, sir. Here is your key. You have locker 313 for the day," he said, presenting Nicholas with a small, antique, brass key. "I've already shined your shoes, and your clothes have been hung up. Is there anything else I can do for you?" he asked.

"No", Nicholas said in surprise as he headed to his locker to change shoes. *Oh, that's right. I should tip the locker room attendant*, Nicholas thought as he arrived at the polished mahogany locker. He then fumbled in his wallet for some cash. [Tipping for extra service is a kind gesture. Similar to other areas of life, the amount is dependent on the environment you are in and the task performed.]

After changing his shoes, Nicholas headed out. On his way, he passed the attendant. "Here you are, Earl. Thank you", Nicholas said as he handed the attendant a tip.

"You are most welcome. Have a great round."

Once outside, Nicholas saw a long row of golf bags on the other side of the sidewalk, leaning against a gleaming brass railing. He quickly spotted his golf bag and let out a small sigh as it stood out from the others. His bag wasn't in poor shape, but it didn't have that new expensive look that the other golf bags did. The bags were adjacent to the driving range, each marking a spot for a golfer to practice and warm up.

As he entered the range he took the area directly in front of his bag. [Driving ranges can have many people practicing at the same time. For the protection of you and others, always stay in the designated hitting areas.] On the right side of his spaced area was half a pyramid of golf balls. Each section had their own stack. [Each range is different. You may need to get your own basket of balls from a machine, a cashier, a large can, or by some other means. If unsure how to proceed, just ask the staff for assistance.]

Some of the stacks were missing a few balls, others were completely emptied. To the front and back of each area was a gold colored rope that ran the length of the practice area. [Do not hit behind or in front of roped-off areas. This is for the safety of you and other golfers as well as for care of the course.]

Nicholas began to warm up with his 9-iron, taking a few practice swings at first. Then, gently, he took a few balls from the top of the stack and laid them on the grass to his side and began hitting them towards the many targets on the range, marked by flags. [Make sure to only hit towards approved areas in the correct direction. Some courses have different rules depending on the type of club you're using. A different section of the range may be designated only for the driver or long iron use versus another may only be for short iron shots.]

"Oops", said Nicholas, taking a big divot on one of his swings. [Divots are okay, and expected, to be taken on grass practice areas. Don't worry, the grounds crew will take care of these at the end of the day. If your divot lies in the practice area you can replace it. Doing so will save the staff time in repairing the damage.] His ball only traveled a foot past the front of his hitting area. [The front of the hitting area should not be crossed, even a little. This boundary is set for safety reasons, as not everyone hits the ball straight or far.] Continuing his practice, Nicholas worked through the stack of balls as he changed clubs every few swings. [Good advice

RICHARD E. TODD

for warming up is to cycle through your clubs, starting with the shortest clubs and moving on to the longest club, the driver, changing clubs every couple balls.] He was also careful to set each ball near the same spot prior to hitting it. [Taking your practice strokes so that your divots overlap by hitting the same area will minimize the turf damage.]

Once he felt he was warmed up, he grabbed his wedge, his putter, and a couple golf balls and headed to the adjacent putting green. [Not all putting greens allow chipping. Look for signs that forbid this action.]

The practice putting green was very large and perfectly manicured. Nicholas pulled the golf balls from his pants pocket and dropped them on the ground near one of the many holes and began practicing short putts.

To one side of the practice putting area an older gentleman was hitting ball after ball to a hole about twenty feet away. He had a dozen golf balls next to him, and there were at least that many around the hole he was aiming at. [You should only use, at most, a couple golf balls when on the practice green.]

In another area, two individuals were each putting towards the same flag, their balls rolling past each other intermittently. [Be respectful in sharing a practice cup, you don't want to hit someone else's ball nor confuse whose balls are whose. If possible wait until the hole is open, or choose another hole to use].

In a far corner, another player was practicing long chip shots to the opposite end of the practice area. Occasionally, his chips would fly over other balls. [Take care to not hit into areas that other people are in. The last thing you want to do is hit someone.] It appeared he was there some time given the many divot marks directly in front of him. [If you are allowed to practice chip shots make sure to repair any damage you do to the turf.]

In yet another area, a large man was practicing one-foot putts. His body was positioned so that no other person could putt towards the hole. [Don't monopolize a practice cup for long periods of time. Sharing is good manners.]

Feeling physically prepared, Nicholas grabbed his golf bag and headed to the starters house that was adjacent to the putting green. [After you pay your green fees, and when ready to start your round, check in with the starter. They are responsible for assuring each group begins in a timely manner and are sufficiently spaced apart from each other.]

RICHARD E. TODD

"READY TO PLAY, lad?" the starter asked as Nicholas approached.

"I am," replied Nicholas.

"Excellent. Your name, please."

"Nicholas Filler."

The starter ran his finger along his clipboard, stopping halfway down the page.

"Right. You will be in a three-man group today, playing with one of our club members, Charles Todd Hound III, and another guest, Mr. William Roberts," he said, pointing to some golfers just a few yards away.

"One of our lads here will put your bag on Mr. Roberts' cart. [When you are a guest it's best you ride in the passenger seat of the golf cart, and not the driver's seat. The member of the club will know the course, the paths, and the cart etiquette better and be in a position to provide guidance. When neither golfer is a member try to default to who is more knowledgeable about the course or golfing etiquette.] There are two groups ahead of you, then we'll get you off.

Any questions?"

"Yes. What are the yardage markers on the course and is there anything special I need to know before playing today," Nicholas responded. [Knowing the course layout is your responsibility. This helps you navigate the course easier and allows you to help others.]

"Our signature flower, the holly bush, can be found on each hole, and serves as our 150-yard marker. There are additional yardage markers in the center of the fairways and on the cart paths at 200, 100, and 50 yards. We've had some nasty weather lately, and not all the holes are thoroughly dry, so watch for signs about cart access. [Occasionally, a course will not allow carts to be driven off the cart paths, or only allow them off the road with certain restrictions, such as 90 degree access onto the fairways. This is done for care of the course.] We also have one fairway that was damaged in the recent storm; there are special instructions at that tee box. [A course may have temporary and non-standard instructions for play throughout the course in order to protect the grounds from further damage or to increase pace of play. Always follow any such instructions.] Any other questions?"

"None. Thank you," Nicholas said as he headed off to meet his group.

"Hi, I'm Nicholas. I'll be in your group today." [Always introduce yourself when playing with unknown people.]

"Wonderful," Charles stated through pursed lips.

"Welcome, partner," said William. "Call me Billy, everyone does. Ready for some great golf for a great cause?" [Take note of your playing partner's names. This will help in addressing them later.]

"Absolutely. I'm looking forward to it. This is my first time on this course." [Letting others know your ability level will set the tone for the round before it starts, so there are no misconceptions later, and can help provide a more relaxed experience during your round.]

"Well yee haw. We're gonna have some fun," Billy replied. "Where do you normally hit from?"

"The white tee markers," replied Nicholas. [Always choose the correct set of tee boxes to hit from. This is dependent on your skill level and how far you drive the ball. Choosing the appropriate tee box will help your game to be more enjoyable.]

"Me too. I'm about a five handicap. What do you say, slim?" Billy stated, looking at Charles.

"My USGA approved index is 1.1 and I'll be playing from the blue tee markers." [Don't let someone intimidate you to hit from a set of tees farther back than is proper for your level of play. There's no award for taking on additional yards, it can increase your score and create frustration to you and those you play with.] I'm a member here at Fox Hunters Country Club and play this course at least three times a week. My name is Charles, and I'm a direct descendent of one of the founders of this club."

"Well ok, Chuck." Billy said.

"Hound group, you're up next," yelled the starter.

"That's us, boys. Let's get this rodeo started," Billy stated as he sat in the golf cart and started it. "Hop in Nicholas," he said before driving towards the white tee box.

Once out of the cart, Nicholas pulled a few golf balls

and some extra tees out of his golf bag. He placed a few in his pockets and the rest in the holders in the cart. [You need to be prepared to keep play moving. Other items that are generally needed are ball markers and a divot repair tool.]

"All clear, Mr. Hound. You may swing away," the starter said. [On the first tee, a starter will generally give you permission when you can begin. This is done to create a safe distance between groups of golfers.]

Charles then teed up his ball from the furthest set of tees and swung, placing a beautiful draw down the middle of the fairway. [If someone is hitting from a tee box further back than you, they are to hit first. This is done for safety reasons.]

The starter then walked over to Charles and, ever so quietly, spoke to him. "I do apologize, Mr. Hound, but due to the relaxed nature of this event and the fact many other participants are not at the level of play of our club members, we will not be playing the blue tees today. I request you play the rest of the round from the white tee markers, if that would be acceptable."

"Fine," said Charles curtly and walked off the tee box. [Course committees can make special rules for specific events, based on that day's weather, work being performed on the course, or for many other reasons. This is done to create a better playing experience or to protect the course for future rounds. Whatever the reason, always follow the 'local rules'.]

"Nice shot, Chuck. Come on Nicholas, let's see what damage we can do. I've played here before, so I'll lead the way for you," Billy said as he teed his ball in the white tee box and started his pre-shot routine. [On the first tee, order of play is decided randomly, by lot. You are welcome to pass the honor onto another, though.] "Just hit it out there in the middle of the fairway, even with them ivy bushes. It's about 250 yards to that point," he said as he took his swing and smacked his drive right where he had indicated. "Yee haw. You're up."

Nicholas started to tee his ball when he saw Charles driving down the cart path towards his ball. [You should wait to leave the teeing ground until everyone in your group has hit. This is done both for etiquette and for safety.]

"Looks like Charles is in a hurry," Billy stated as he stood directly to the right side of Nicholas' ball as Nicholas prepared to play. [You should not stand even with the person hitting, nor behind or in front. This is done so it doesn't cause a distraction to the person about to swing and prevents you from being hit by the ball or the club. Also, do not stand so that you are looking down the line of play of the person hitting as this too is distracting to the player. The best advice is to stand off to the side and behind the ball.]

Taking a deep breath and exhaling to relieve his stress, Nicholas took his turn and drove the ball down the fairway, stopping twenty yards short of Billy's and towards the right side of the fairway.

"That'll do," said Billy, moving towards the cart.

Nicholas reached down, grabbed his tee, and followed. [Picking up your tee, broken or not, will keep the tee box clear for other golfers.]

Even though the first hole, a 397 yard par-4, was an easy opening stretch, being nearly straight with a tree lined out of bounds on the left and only a few sparsely growing maple trees on the right, Nicholas was glad to get through the first tee jitters and keep his ball in play.

The cart came to a slow stop as they approached Nicholas' ball. [Take care not to start or stop a cart quickly to avoid damage to the course and potential injury to riders.] Nicholas looked at the ball on the ground, searching for the green line he drew on all his golf balls. [You should uniquely mark your ball to assure you don't play someone else's or someone else doesn't play your ball.] After verifying the ball was his, and being furthest away with 170 yards to the green, he hit using his fairway wood. He managed good contact, landing the ball just in front of the green.

Having played from the further tee box, despite the extra distance on his drive, Charles was just outside the holly bushes, at about 160 yards.

"These bushes, Illex opaca, also known as the American Holly, were hand selected by my great, great, great, grandfather to be a symbol on this course of beauty and achievement," Charles stated before calmly taking his 7-iron and landing his shot on the green.

Billy was next. Being even with the holly bushes on either side of the fairway, he knew he was exactly 150 yards to the hole. [Knowing the course layout can help plan your shot and can decrease the time it takes to play.] Playing an 8-iron, his ball landed on the green. "Yippee", he said, as he put his club back in the golf bag and sat in the golf cart.

Billy parked the cart a few yards next to the green, just off the cart path. [Never drive near, or on, the putting green. This can cause damage to the turf.] Nicholas exited and grabbed his wedge and his putter and headed to his ball.

RICHARD E. TODD

[Taking your putter, along with any other currently needed clubs, saves you from not having to go back to the cart after hitting, and keeps the pace of play moving]. Nicholas then chipped onto the green, his ball stopping ten feet from the hole.

Charles was already standing on the green, cleaning his ball with a small white towel. He then set his ball next to the marker on the ground and started lining up his putt. [You must mark your ball on the green before you can lift it and clean it]. He had a lengthy putt and ran it a foot past the right side of the cup.

"Not bad, Chuck," Billy said who was now furthest away. [Whoever is farthest from the hole putts next.] Lining up his putt, Billy stroked it, leaving it a couple inches short.

"Good enough for me," Billy said as he took his putter and flipped the ball into the air and caught it. [All putts should be holed out. That is to say, you should continue to putt until the ball rests in the bottom of the cup.]

He then remained standing near the hole, waiting for Nicholas to finish. [Don't stand in such a manner that it might cause a distraction or an obstruction to someone putting.]

Nicholas was next to putt. His first stroke left the ball two feet short of the cup. He then walked up to the ball, reset his stance, and stroked it in the cup. "Shweh," he said as he picked his ball out of the cup and walked to the side of the green.

"That's a gimmie, Chuck," Billy stated, referring to Charles' short distance between his ball and the cup. [A 'gimmie' is a conceded putt, usually a very short and makeable shot. This is done to keep the pace of play moving and to relieve a little pressure of having to make every putt. This is not a legal action in regulation stroke play.]

"I play out all my shots," Charles replied as he lined up his short putt and sank it. "Par," he said. "Why don't I be our marker for this round?" [A 'marker' is the person designated to keep the official score for each golfer in a group. Every golfer may keep their own totals or have their own marker, but it's easy to have one person handle this task.]

"Fine by me," Billy said.

"So that's even for me and Mr. Roberts, and one over for Mr. Filler," Charles stated as he pulled out a pencil and the scorecard from his pocket and filled in the results while standing over the hole. [You should mark the scores off the green or on the tee box of the next hole. This helps speed the pace of play by allowing those playing behind you to hit onto the green rather than wait while you to finish and exit the green.]

"Tally ho, gentlemen. Off to the next hole," Charles stated and he started toward his cart.

RICHARD E. TODD

A SHORT DRIVE led to the tee box of the 2ⁿᵈ hole. The teeing area for this par-3 was set on the plateau of the top of a steep hill, 135 yards from the green. A small pond bordered part of the front and the entire right side of the putting area. A wooded out-of-bounds line ran along the left side of the fairway, and a bunker was positioned on the left side of the green.

Charles teed his ball and let loose a smooth 9-iron. The ball sailed into the sky and seemed to take forever to fall, eventually landing on the front of the green.

With a small smile at his well hit shot, Charles picked up his tee. Finding it was broken, he simply tossed it back on the ground. [If your tee breaks, pick up the pieces and properly dispose of them in a trash can or waste bin. These containers are normally found near the tee box on each hole. This saves others from picking up after you and diminishes wear and tear on mowers.]

Billy then set his ball and started his pre-shot routine.

"Did you like that shot?" Charles asked as Billy began

his backswing. [Be quiet when someone else is preparing to hit. It's rude and a distraction to talk when another person is playing a shot.]

Not allowing the comment to break his concentration, Billy swung his 8-iron, landing his ball on the right side of the green, just five feet from the flagstick.

"I did, but I liked mine more," he stated.

Nicholas played last, teeing off with his 7-iron.

"That's looking good," Billy stated, as Nicholas' ball headed on a path for the green. [You shouldn't comment on ball flight until it is clear where the ball is going or where it will land. Having to take back a compliment when someone has a bad shot just makes matters worse.]

Unfortunately, the swing was a little off center and the ball faded to the left and landed in the sand trap. [The technical name for a sand trap is hazard.]

"Bad luck, old man," Charles stated as he headed down to the green.

Nicholas arrived at the bunker, took his sand wedge, and entered. Addressing his ball he slowly dug his feet into the sand for a solid stance. [Digging into the sand with your feet is acceptable and often necessary.]

While waiting for Nicholas to play, Billy and Charles had time to line up their putts. [When waiting for someone else to play, take the time to prepare for your next shot.]

A big swing launched his ball, and a handful of sand, into the air. The ball, ever so softly, settled onto the green, seven feet from the flagstick.

"Nice out," Billy stated. [Compliments on a well-played shot are always welcome, but don't overdo it.]

Nicholas, now on the green, was still furthest away from the cup but wasn't able to quickly get to his ball for his next shot as he still had to rake the bunker, retrieve his putter, and walk onto the green.

With everyone's golf ball on the green, Billy promptly pulled the flag out of the cup, set it on the ground out of the way, and headed back to his ball. [Whoever is closest to the hole should tend the flagstick.]

Taking a few steps to the side, Nicholas grabbed a rake and smoothed out his footprints and the impact area from his swing as he walked out of the hazard. [Always leave the bunker in better condition than you found it. This will assure the next player has as much opportunity to hit out of the sand as you did.] Once done, he set the rake on the grass outside the bunker. [There are many best practices on what to do with a rake. Some say the rake should be inside the bunker, while others say outside, but it should always be parallel with the fairway. Each course has different preferred ways to handle rake replacement so check the local rules. Another suggestion is to leave the rake where you found it.] Nicholas then took his club and struck it against his shoes before walking away. [You should always knock the sand off your shoes with your club so you don't track debris onto the green. This will help to maintain a smooth putting surface.]

Rather than wait longer, Charles, with a straight up-hill lie, stroked his putt. [Being prepared to hit when the opportunity presents itself helps speed up the round. The rules of golf say it is okay to play out of turn, without penalty.] The slant was too much, and the putt stopped on the lip. Charles then walked up and tapped it in the cup.

"Bully," he said, as he walked over and picked his ball out of the cup.

"Are you ready?" Billy asked Nicholas.

"Just a second," he replied. "If you are ready then go ahead and hit." [If you are prepared to play and it's not your turn, just ask each player if they are ready to play. This is a friendly way of keeping the game moving without insulting the others' honor for turn.]

With that, Billy played, leaving his breaking putt for birdie a foot short, which he then hit in for par. "Yee hah," he said.

Nicholas, ready to play, lined up his putt and put a nice roll on it. The downhill lie threw off his line and the ball ran a foot past. He then walked over and ran it back and into the hole.

"There ya go," Billy said, as Nicholas pulled his ball and Billy's ball out of the cup. [You should remove your ball after you hole out, which is golf speak for finishing the hole, before others hole their own putt. Having your ball in the cup could determine how other player's shots are affected.]

"Thanks. Here you are," Nicholas said, handing Billy his golf ball, as each player headed to the next green.

3
Chapter

BILLY AND NICHOLAS watched as Charles walked
to the tee box for his drive on the par-4 3rd hole. He
seemed to take forever as he teed up a ball, and performed
several practice swings before slowly taking his address and
finally sending the ball on a straight shot down the left side
of the fairway, fifty yards short of the green. [You can play
at your own pace, but try not to cause an excessive delay for
your group.]

"You're turn, gents," he said as he slipped a head-cover
over his driver and returned it to his golf bag.

"I'm not ready," Billy said to Nicholas, "Why don't you
go ahead and hit." [Even in the tee box you may play out of
order in friendly matches. This decreases the waiting time
between players.]

"Ok," said Nicholas, as he grabbed his club, stepped up
to the teeing area, and began his pre-shot routine. [A pre-
shot routine helps put you in the mindset to hit a consistent
shot, but remember to keep it short to avoid long delays and
to keep the momentum going.] A quick couple waggles and

Nicholas swung. The ball's path started down the center of the fairway then slowly drifted to the sparsely tree-lined right side that ran parallel to the oncoming 16th fairway, then it landed and rolled further into the wooded area.

"Did anyone see where it stopped?" asked Nicholas.

"It's your ball, not mine," stated Charles. [You should help your fellow players by watching their shots. In turn, they will help you. This increases the pace of play and decreases the stress of searching for your ball.]

"Sorry, pal, I lost it as it crossed the cart path. It's gotta be in them trees," Billy replied, as he prepared for his shot.

"Great," replied Nicholas sullenly.

"Time for Saturday church," Billy said as he stepped into the tee box. "You know, hit it and pray," he explained upon seeing Nicholas' confused expression. Billy's drive headed on the same path as Nicholas'. "Looks like I'm going to join you," he said, as they watched the ball's flight, landing near the right side of the fairway in the first cut of rough before bouncing. "Although I'm not exactly sure where it stopped," Billy continued.

"It's at the base of the third tree," Nicholas said. [See how watching each other's ball path helps?]

"Thanks. Let's go get 'em," Billy said as he and Nicholas headed down the fairway.

Charles reached his ball promptly. He was alone and on the opposite side of the fairway from the others and was prepared for his second shot, while Nicholas and Billy searched for Nicholas' ball. Despite being closest to the hole, he played. [Normal procedure states whoever is farthest from the hole is to play next. This is not as important in the fairway as it is on the tee box or on the putting green. Playing when ready, provided others are not ready nor in the way, keeps the game moving.] A short little wedge put Charles' ball on the front side of the green, leaving him a ten-foot uphill putt.

"Here ya go, partner," Billy said, pointing to a ball between two trees.

"Thanks," replied Nicholas. "You're by that tree," he said, pointing up ahead a few yards.

Nicholas pulled out his sand wedge, hoping to fly the ball through the tree branches and over a bunker that separated his ball and the cup, and began setting up his swing.

"I think you should use a lower lofted iron and punch it to the side of the green to avoid that trap," Billy stated. [Unless you are asked, don't provide your advice on play. It's rude and you can be penalized as this is an infraction of the rules of golf. This is covered in the previous book of *The Golf Rules* series.]

Paying no attention, Nicholas swung, sending his ball on a high arc to the green. The ball caught a small branch on its flight which sent it directly down into the sand.

"Them's the breaks," Billy said, as he pitched his ball onto the backside of the green to set himself up for a long, downhill putt.

Once into the bunker, Nicholas played a great shot, dropping the ball softly onto the putting green just five feet from the hole.

"That's a nice out, kid," Billy shouted while Nicholas raked the bunker. Billy then pulled his putter from his golf bag and headed to his ball.

"Thanks," Nicholas replied as he walked to the green, marked his ball, picked it up, grabbed the flagstick and stepped out of Charles' line of putt, setting the flag to the side of the action.

Charles, having had ample time to prepare, was ready to putt. [When waiting for others you should prepare for your next shot. This keeps the action going when it becomes your turn to play.] Addressing his ball he looked back and forth from the ball to the cup. "Kindly step to the side, Mr. Roberts. Your shadow is interfering with my line of sight." [Polite requests are how situations should be handled.]

"Sorry, Chuck," Billy said, taking a big side step. [You should not stand on another player's line, nor cast your shadow in a way that interferes with the player's stroke.]

With a firm swing Charles let it roll. The putt looked good; however, it came up a foot short.

"Hmm," stated Charles, as he walked up to his ball and tapped it in. "That's par for me," he said as he extracted a pipe from his vest pocket before retrieving his ball. [You should take care of your personal tasks when others are not waiting for you to move.]

Billy tapped his putt ever so gently, sending the ball on a slow but steady path down the slope, eventually finding the bottom of the cup.

"Yeh haw, that's a bird for me," Billy explained as he pulled his ball from the cup.

Nicholas stroked his short putt in for par. "Shwew," he said, as he picked up the flagstick, still lying on the ground, and returned it to the cup. [The first to hole out should be

RICHARD E. TODD

the one to pick up the flag stick and hold it while the rest of the group putts out. This keeps the equipment out of the way of others and cuts down on the time spent cleaning up the green after the group is finished.]

Walking towards the next hole, Nicholas noticed Charles still back on the green, recreating his long uphill putt, this time holing it. "Better," Charles said to himself, picking up his ball. [It's not illegal to practice putting on a hole you just completed but time for practice was before the round started. Don't make the group behind you have to wait more than necessary.]

RICHARD E. TODD

4
Chapter

"LOOKS LIKE I have honors," Billy said with pride as he prepared for his drive on the 350 yard par-4. The fairway was wide and straight, with trees lining both sides.

As Billy started to set his tee a grounds crew member was spotted driving a utility cart down the left side of the fairway, picking up small branches.

"If you keep your drive in the fairway he won't be a problem," stated Charles. "He knows the risks of his job." [The greens staff should be respected and protected. Give them a minute to finish the work they are doing, and they will usually move out of your way and be very grateful to you for not hitting at them. Remember, the grounds crew keeps the course in its beautiful state for your enjoyment.]

"I'll give 'em a minute," responded Billy as he stepped back and took a couple of practice strokes while the cart continued on its way down the fairway and off to the next hole.

Billy then addressed the ball and sent it on a perfect

flight, fading slightly and coming to rest just past the patch of holly bushes near the right side of the fairway, adjacent to the cart path. "I'll take it. Let's see what you can do, Chuck."

Charles responded with an explosive drive, sending his ball down the left side. "Drat," he said as everyone watched the ball hit the fairway and dart into the sparsely wooded area that separated the fairway from the out of bounds line.

"I'm sure you'll find that, Mr. Hound," Nicholas said comfortingly as he headed to the tee box. [Bad shots happen to everyone. You don't have to give reassuring comments on each one, especially if your playing partner is not a close friend.]

A quick waggle and Nicholas' drive was off, his ball settling on the same line but some distance behind Billy's.

Once to his lie, Nicholas found he had 125 yards to the thin, long, and sloped green. He hoped to land it on the front edge, near the flagstick, to avoid a long and downhill putt. A smooth 8-iron placed his ball just short of the green but in a good location to save par. Glancing to the left he saw Charles, driving his cart up and down the edge of the fairway, still looking for his ball. Nicholas promptly put his club back in his golf bag and headed across the fairway to assist in the search. [It's good manners to help others search for lost balls during their round, especially those in your group. This encourages a friendly spirit and helps with pace of play.]

Billy then hit on, his ball coming to rest at the back half of the green.

After a quick walk through the trees, Nicholas called out, "Here's your ball, Mr. Hound," pointing down at the ground. [If the ball can't be found quickly and there are other golfers ready to play but are waiting on you, and the area in front of you is open, then the group behind you should be offered to play through. [The rules of golf define five minutes as the maximum time allowed to look for a lost ball.]]

Without a word, Charles grabbed his wedge and hit his ball onto the back of the green, then headed back to his cart. [Obviously, a 'thank you' is always in order when you receive help.]

Seeing Charles leave Nicholas by himself, Billy drove across the fairway to give him a ride to the green. [If time allows, and the act would be of help without undue delay of play, you can drive others to their next shots.]

Nicholas and Billy drove off and parked on the right side of the green, just off the cart path. Nicholas pulled out a 9-iron and his putter and headed to his ball. [It's a good idea to take all the clubs you may need, so you don't have to walk back and forth from your lie to your golf bag. This is another playing pace item that shows respect for everyone's time.]

Nicholas was preparing for a straight twenty-foot chip to the cup when Charles pulled up right next to him, parked his cart, grabbed his putter, and walked to the back of the green. [Always be courteous not to create a distraction when someone is preparing to hit.]

A short chip by Nicholas left his ball a foot from the hole. Nicholas then walked to the green, pulled the flag stick out and gently set it to the side of the green along with his wedge, then tapped his ball in for par. [Be cautious when setting down any equipment on the green. The grass can easily be damaged, which creates an unpleasant experience for other players and extra work for groundskeepers].

Charles was lining up his long, downhill putt while Billy was fixing his ball mark and other marks he found on the green. [Care for the course, not just the damage you cause, increases the enjoyment for all players]. A smooth stroke sent the ball on a line for the cup. Not having the speed needed, it finished a foot short. Charles then tapped in and headed to his cart. [To decrease distractions while others are putting, and to show respect for your fellow competitors, stay on the green until everyone has holed out.]

Billy also two putt to earn another par. "Yea haw," he said, "pars all around."

"Good hole," Nicholas said as he grabbed the flagstick, replaced it in the cup, and headed to the cart.

"Hey, you forgot your wedge," Billy stated, pointing behind Nicholas. [Help your partners and competitors when you can for you may need them to help you.]

"Thanks," Nicholas said as he darted back to retrieve the club. [A good tip is to leave extra clubs on or near a pulled flagstick so they aren't forgotten.]

RICHARD E. TODD

I T WAS A short drive through the woods to the 5th hole. The tee box was nestled back into a clearing in the trees, creating a wooded chute for drives on this short par-4.

"You still have the honors, Mr. Roberts," Nicholas stated.

"Just a moment," Billy responded, his foot resting on the tee marker while he was tying his shoe. [Do not take an action that can cause damage to the course. You may only be there a few hours but many other golfers will follow you. Keep the course in great shape.]

"All set," Billy said, then he teed and addressed his ball. He had just begun his backswing as Charles rejoined the group, bringing his golf cart to an abrupt halt, causing the loose gravel to spray about. [Do not cause a distraction when another player is ready to hit. It breaks their concentration, and you wouldn't like it if it were done to you.]

"Do you mind, Chuck? I'm ready to hit," Billy stated.

"My apologies old man. Have at it," Charles responded, to which Billy let fly his drive.

After the ball passed through the narrow opening it found itself sailing in an open area, flying alongside a slow flowing creek, moving closer to the hole on a gentle fade, and finally coming to rest on the opposite side of the fairway near the trees that separated this hole from the previous one.

"I like that," Billy commented on his drive as he grabbed his tee and headed off the tee box.

Charles took his respective turn, placing his drive down the middle of the fairway, just past Billy's ball. "I like that even better," he said as Nicholas took his place on the tee box. [There's nothing wrong with friendly competition, but make sure it stays that way. There's no need for negative talk on the course.]

After a quick waggle, Nicholas swung, sending the ball on a fast hook and into the stream.

"Damn," he mumbled as he slammed his driver into the ground. [Anger is no reason to damage any part of the course.] "That's my mulligan for the day," he stated as he grabbed another ball from his pocket to re-tee. [Remember, a 'mulligan', or re-do or do-over, is not a legal option. Every stroke must be counted.]

"We count every stroke, Mr. Filler," stated Charles. "That's the way a gentleman plays."

"You're right," replied Nicholas, who then released a deep breath and took a gentle swing at his replacement ball, landing it in the center of the fairway some twenty yards short of the familiar holly bush. He then reached down and, using his tee, repaired the impression in the ground he made in anger with his club. [Errors in judgment happen, just remember to correct them if you can.]

RICHARD E. TODD

Reaching his lie and still away, Nicholas played an 8-iron which landed his ball just short of the green.

Billy played next, landing his wedge in one of the hazards that protected the front sides of the green.

Charles smoothly landed his wedge shot on the back of the green, providing him a slightly downhill, ten-foot putt.

Walking across the green, Billy came to the deep bunker where his ball lay. "Yea haw," he yelled as he jumped down into the sand to prepare for his shot. [You should enter and exit a bunker gently and on the low side or where indicated by stairs or paths.]

Charles, being the only one on the green and having a few minutes while he waited for the rest of his group to hit onto the green, retrieved the pipe from his golf bag. Standing over his ball he lit it and started blowing smoke about. In that brief moment, between inhale and exhale, Charles jumped and choked as he was sprayed with sand from the blast that came out of the bunker as Billy's ball was lofted onto the green, coming to rest within several feet of the cup. [When hitting onto the green or out of a bunker, always alert other players that are nearby or in the possible line of flight.]

"Sorry, Chuck," stated Billy as he drug his wedge back and forth to smooth out the sand before exiting the bunker. [Always use the rake provided to put the bunker in the same, or better, condition you found it.]

Nicholas played a short chip from the front of the green, his ball stopping five feet from the cup.

Charles, being next to play, tapped his pipe against his overly polished golf shoes, spilling smoking ash about on the green. [You aren't the only person that will be playing that hole. Keep it clean and free of foreign objects. No one wants to putt through ash or debris.) He then took his line and sent the ball on its path. All eyes watched the ball slowly trickle down the hill as it came closer and closer to the hole until it finally stopped, a few inches from the cup. Walking up to the ball, Charles hit it in with a one handed putt.

"Bully," stated Charles, then pulled his ball from the cup, having earned par.

Billy two-putt for bogey while Nicholas scored a double-bogey six, due to the penalty for hitting his ball into the water. [You should always count your penalty strokes. Tacking on a penalty doesn't make you any worse or better golfer, it's just playing by the rules so that everyone is playing the same game. This also protects your integrity as no one can call you a cheat.]

"Hey, is that your club," Nicholas asked, pointing to the opposite side of the green, just in the short rough. [When setting your club down while playing a different one, try to not leave it in the rough. Clubs are easily forgotten when they aren't clearly visible. A tip is to leave your club on or near the putting green.]

"Not mine," replied Billy.

"Ok, I'll grab it," he said then went to it, picked it up, and inspected it. [It's a good idea to mark your clubs with some identification so you can be contacted if you lose one.] "Maybe it's the group ahead of us." [If you find a club, pick it up. Try to ask the group ahead of you at the next tee, or when you see them, if the club belongs to them. If you can't find the owner then return it to the clubhouse.]

RICHARD E. TODD

A S NICHOLAS REACHED the 6ᵗʰ tee box he saw the group that was playing in front of them. They had just finished teeing off and were leaving the tee box.

"Anyone missing a wedge," he yelled to them.

"Yeah, that's mine," explained one of the golfers after reviewing his golf bag. "Thanks a lot," he said, taking the club from Nicholas. [You can look out for other players on the course too, not just those in your group. You'd want them to do the same for you, especially when it comes to your favorite and expensive clubs.]

"No problem," Nicholas said, then walked back to his group.

"Now that your good deed is done, it's my turn, chaps," Charles exclaimed as he dropped a ball onto the teeing area to prepare for the 135 yard par-3. "Best to be short on this hole. That green has a devil of a slant," he said before letting fly a pitching wedge to the front edge of the putting green, providing him a straight, uphill putt of eleven feet. [Giving advice is presumptuous. Keep it to yourself.]

As Billy prepared for his shot he abruptly stopped as he watched another player briskly walk across the center of the fairway. Apparently this golfer's shot, from another hole, was offline and crossed over into a different fairway. This golfer quickly hit his ball, threw up a hand as a 'thank you', and darted back to his proper fairway. [Mishit shots often find their way onto other fairways. Help others by giving them non-dangerous conditions to pick up or play their ball.]

Regaining his focus, Billy stroked a 9-iron and landed his golf ball in the center of the green, but the slope was too steep, and the ball rolled down the putting green and off into the fairway. "Yup, you were right, Chuck," Billy said as his ball came to rest past Charles' ball.

Last to hit, Nicholas landed his tee shot short of the green, ten feet behind Charles.

Billy drove up to Nicholas' ball and let him out of the cart then drove behind the green and parked on the cart path. [Driving a player to his ball and dropping him off provides that player time to prepare for his shot while the other player either parks the cart or goes to their own ball location.]

Being some twenty yards out, but having a good lie on short grass, Nicholas used his 7-iron to putt the ball. His efforts did put the ball on the green but left it eight feet short of the cup.

Billy, being in a similar position, also used his 7-iron but ended only five feet from the cup.

Charles hit next, leaving his putt on the lip of the cup.

"That's good enough for me," Billy stated, hitting

Charles' ball back to him before pulling the flag stick from the cup and heading towards his own lie. [Don't hit another player's ball or take from them the opportunity to hole their own putt. It makes such a nice sound when it falls into the cup!]

Nicholas sent his putt towards the hole. Miscalculating the speed needed to go up the hill, he left it a foot short. He promptly tapped it in for bogey.

Despite Billy's putt being short, it was difficult due to having a tough break in the green. He lined up his ball and stroked it towards the hole. He had the line, but the speed was off, and the ball missed the hole by a half inch and rolled down the green another yard. Taking his stance again, he was able to sink his putt. "Dang. I bogeyed that hole," he said.

"Tough hole for you two gents," Charles said with a smirk as he walked off the green, having earned par and a stroke on each of them. [It's most courteous to always be positive and not condescending in talking with other players and competitors. Golf is a game of honor.]

RICHARD E. TODD

7
Chapter

"IF ONLY THAT putt had gone an inch further out. I would have had a birdie instead of a bogey and taken the honors," Billy declared, speaking about the last hole. [Don't dwell on previous shots or what might have been. The past is over, golf is not a game of perfect, and no one wants to hear about your 'almost' stories.]

"That's the way the ball falls, Mr. Roberts, or doesn't fall in your case," Charles chortled as he teed up his ball for the 7th hole, which ran along the edge of the golf course property. He took aim at the holly bush on the left side of the fairway, which marked the beginning of the severe dogleg that bent to the right to split this 390 yard par-4 in half.

While waiting his turn, Nicholas stood at the back of the tee box. Leaning on his driver as it were a fence. [Acts like this can break or bend your clubs, cause injury to yourself, and potentially damage the turf.]

A smooth swing sent Charles' ball on a direct path towards the out of bounds line. Landing on the edge of the fairway, the ball rolled into the light rough under a large oak tree near some homes that bordered the course.

Billy, still fuming about the last hole, quickly teed a ball and released some of his anger with a swing that was forced more than fluid, causing the ball to slice and land in the sparse, young pine trees that provided protection from golfers trying to cut the dogleg. "Dangnabit," he said.

Nicholas, seeing the best and worst scenarios, played a 3-wood to the center of the fairway but short of the others.

Preparing for his second shot of 155-yards, a smooth 5-iron landed Nicholas' ball on the left side of the green, pin high. "Yes," he exclaimed to himself.

Glancing to the right, he watched Billy driving the cart in and out of the pine trees, letting his foot hang out of the cart and drag along the grass, while as he looked for his ball. [This is a dangerous action as you can be injured. As they say at the amusement parks, "Keep your arms and legs inside the ride at all times."]

As Nicholas headed to assist in the search, Billy stopped the cart, stepped out, and grabbed a club. [Always be ready to help another golfer.] Addressing a ball on the ground, he managed to hit it through and over the troublesome trees and onto the front of the green.

Once to his ball, Charles noticed another golf ball nearby that was past the out of bounds marker and in one of the home's backyards. He glanced around to see if anyone was watching. Seeing none, he quickly stepped over a "no trespassing" sign and grabbed the ball. "Ahh, my same brand," he said as he darted back to the fairway. [Some courses will have private homes nearby. Respect their

RICHARD E. TODD

privacy and stay off of their land.] With a full wedge, he also landed his ball on the front of the green, just in front of Billy's. Getting back in his cart, he drove right up to the front of the green so that he had but a few steps to his ball. [Another way to care for the putting green is to keep carts off and a suitable distance away. Generally, you'll see small signs that direct carts away from the green.]

Charles bent down and, with a smooth motion, picked up his ball then dropped a ball marker on the spot where his ball had been, then began to clean his ball. [The rules state you are to mark the ball then pick it up, not the other way around. By not following this order you will incur a one stroke penalty (rule 20-1). Follow this procedure exactly so your fellow players can't state you didn't replace the ball in the same spot.]

While waiting for the others to putt, Nicholas fixed his ball mark, and several others he found on the green from previous players. [Fixing your own ball marks is the least you should do. Take the time to see if you can fix other indentations so as to leave the putting green in better condition than you found it.]

"Go ahead, old man. You're away," Charles said to Billy.

As Billy addressed his ball and prepared to putt, Charles sidled up behind him to get a read on the break. [You shouldn't stand behind someone putting, or in front of them on their line, in order to find the break of the putt. It's best to stand to the side or away from them as to not cause a distraction nor be obvious about your intention.] He had the line but didn't give it enough power to make it up the hill, leaving it three inches short. Trudging up to the ball, he tapped it in. "Still saved par," he said.

Charles, having seen Billy's error, stroked his putt harder than he thought he needed to although it still wasn't enough, leaving the ball an inch short before hitting it in with his next stroke.

Now his turn, Nicholas rolled his putt. Misjudging the break, he left it short. A quick tap and he was in for par, too.

RICHARD E. TODD

8

Chapter

CHARLES LED OFF the group by placing his drive in the middle of the straight par-4 fairway, which set him up for a 100 yard approach to the tiered green that was surrounded by several large clumps of very tall sea oats.

Billy hit next, sending his ball to the right, just off the fairway but short of the sparse pine trees he had just been in on the last hole.

Nicholas leaked his drive to the left side of the fairway, near a lone, young Maple tree, even with Billy.

Billy and Nicholas, reaching their lies at the same time, looked at each other to see who was away and should play next. There was an awkward moment as each waited for the other to play as it wasn't clear who was further out. Billy broke the stare off, "Go ahead and hit if you're ready." [When in doubt as to who should hit, it's friendly to offer the option to play next to your playing partner or competitor.]

Nicholas took the offer and addressed his ball. Being in a good lie and 150 yards from the green, he played a 5-iron for his second shot. A big swing sent the ball flying toward the green, followed by a large divot being sent into the air. The ball landed on the fairway and rolled onto the front of the green, leaving him a long, twenty foot, up-hill putt.

"Nice," Nicholas said to himself as he walked forward, grabbed the clump of grass he dislodged, returned it to its original spot, and tamped it down with his foot. [Another way to care for the course is to always repair your divots. This may require more work than simply replacing some sod and patting it down].

Billy also had an unobstructed path to the green. His stroke made solid contact with the ball, sending it towards the putting green, but the bottom of his swing arc was too low, and he heaved a large amount of grass and dirt about. Looking at the area in front of him and the remnants that was the grass his ball had been sitting on, there was nothing worth saving. He quickly went to the golf cart and grabbed the bottle of seed mixture then returned to the divot area. He poured some of the mixture onto the bare earth and stomped on it. [When the damage done is severe you may be asked to apply grass seed and fertilizer to help with the care of the grounds. If the course provides you with this mixture, please use it when needed. This helps the area heal faster than hoping the grounds crew can find the bare patch and fix it later.]

Charles was standing nearly on top of the 100 yard marker. A nice pitch put his ball at the back of the putting green, on the flat area, seven feet from the hole.

Once to his lie, Nicholas reviewed his line of putt. "I'm concerned I'm going to hit your ball, Billy. It's sitting on my intended path," Nicholas said.

"No problem, partner," Billy responded, as he walked over to his ball, marked it, and picked it up. [On the green you can easily mark your ball so it's not in anyone's line. This makes it easier for them to play and is good sportsmanship and documented in the rules.]

"Thanks," Nicholas said then hit his putt hard, sending it up the long incline and coming to rest on the higher tier, just a yard from the cup.

"Yea haw. Good putt," Billy said, as he lined up his own ball and rolled it with the same speed, coming to rest two feet from the hole.

"Back at ya," Nicholas said.

Charles was away and stroked his putt to within a foot of the cup. Walking up to it, he gently tapped it in for par.

Billy and Nicholas also dropped their putts, holing out for par.

Glancing towards the next hole, Nicholas saw the group ahead of them just waiting to tee off.

"Maybe we should ask them if we can play through," he said to Charles and Billy.

"Naw, ain't no place to go. One more hole and we hit the turn. May as well rest a bit," Billy said. [There are times when the group ahead of you is slower than your group. If this happens, and provided the area in front of the group ahead of you is open, it may be best for everyone on the course for your group to switch places with that group. And there are times when your group might be the ones slowing play for others. There is nothing wrong or impolite about playing through another group, provided it's done with tact and there's a good reason for doing so.]

With some time to spare, Nicholas took a moment to look about and enjoy the surroundings. He saw a cart moving across one of the other fairways. A third person was hanging off the back of the cart. "Kids," he thought. [Do not treat a golf cart in a manner it's not meant. Putting extra stress on the cart can damage the frame or possibly the engine. It also can add too much weight on the turf, causing tire tracks to be embedded in the fairway.]

RICHARD E. TODD

9
Chapter

"MUST BE MY lucky day," Nicholas said, as he walked towards the tee box of the 9th hole. Just off the cart path, he reached down, and picked up a driver head-cover that resembled a shark. "Someone must have forgot to put it back on their club after they teed off", he said, setting it on the dashboard of his golf cart before heading to the back of the tee box to await his turn. [Helping to reunite lost equipment with its owner will be appreciated.]

Charles had honors and placed his drive even, and to the right side, of a massive, old, oak tree that stood in the center of the fairway near the 250 yard marker of the long par-5.

Billy played next, landing his ball twenty yards short of Charles, near the cart path that ran the length of the right side of the fairway.

Nicholas hooked his drive slightly, landing near the tree lined out-of-bounds markers that bordered the left side of the fairway.

At their lies, each player had to again wait for the group ahead to hit and move forward. Once the area was clear,

Nicholas, Billy, and Charles played their second shots. [You should always wait to hit if there is a chance you might reach the group in front of you, even if that chance is slight.]

No one's shot reached the green, but each had a clear chip from inside fifty yards; with Nicholas and Billy near the front of the green and Charles to the right.

As he walked to his ball, Billy watched the group ahead of them finish putting out. This group was walking the course, rather than driving, as evidenced by the golf bags that were lying about on the putting green. [Take care on the putting green as the turf is easily damaged. Don't lay large, heavy, or jagged objects on the putting green to avoid leaving indentations or tearing the turf, and don't carry your golf bag onto the green as the extra weight of the bag can create depressions of your footsteps.]

With the last ball in the hole, this group grabbed their bags and headed to the clubhouse.

As Nicholas came closer to his ball and the putting green, the sound from the clubhouse patio grew louder. [Enjoy yourself, but if others are playing nearby, be courteous.]

Once to his ball, Nicholas started practicing his swing.

"Careful," Billy yelled as he barely avoided being hit on the head by Nicholas' wedge.

"Sorry," Nicholas responded, as he stepped back to let Billy play. [Always assure your area is clear before swinging.]

A simple quarter-swing landed Billy's ball near the hole.

Nicholas then hit his ball to within seven feet of the cup, followed by Charles who chipped his ball to six feet from the cup.

RICHARD E. TODD

Billy walked over, pulled the flagstick, and gently set it to the side, out of everyone's putting line. [Always keep the line of play clear of equipment and people.]

Nicholas rolled his putt, but it stopped a foot short, which he then tapped in. "I'll take par."

Billy's birdie putt ended short before it was tapped in for par. "Yee haw," he said as he fished his putter head into the cup to retrieve his ball. [Using a club to retract your ball from the cup can cause damage to the area around the hole. Always use your hand or a specialty device for retrieving a ball from the cup.]

Charles left his short putt on the lip, earning him par also.

"Good front nine," Nicholas said, as they all headed toward the clubhouse.

"Nice spread," Billy stated as he entered the dining area, referring to the large selection of finger sandwiches, hors d'oeuvre, wines and champagnes, and all served on fine china adorned with the Fox Hunters Country Club crest. He then promptly started filling a plate.

"Rightfully so, but let's not dawdle. Golf and all that, you know," Charles replied as he picked up half of a sandwich and headed back to his cart. [Here's another pace of play situation. You are allowed to stop in the clubhouse for a snack, a drink, or something more substantial, but do so quickly. Some courses will dictate how much time you can spend between the 9th and 10th holes.] "Let's stay ahead of the group behind us." [Being prompt when passing the 9th hole can be advantageous. It could allow your group to stay ahead of a larger or slower group, or can allow you to bypass a slower group, or help keep an open area in front of your group.]

"Looks like we're movin'," Billy said to Nicholas, as both quickly downed a small glass of champagne, grabbed a couple sandwiches, and darted off.

RICHARD E. TODD

ARRIVING AT THE 10th tee box, Charles noticed an unfamiliar two-person group was preparing to tee off.

"I don't recognize you from this morning. Are you with the outing?" he asked, just as Billy and Nicholas pulled up.

"No. We were hoping to jump on the course for a quick nine," one of the new golfers stated.

"Sorry gentlemen, we're in the middle of a round. You may see if there's an opening after us or check with the starter," Charles stated as he pulled his driver from his golf bag and walked onto the teeing ground. [Priority of playing order is given to anyone that is playing 18 holes, over a group just playing nine. Not only is this listed in the USGA's rule book, it's polite so that a group already playing can continue their round uninterrupted.]

A quick waggle and Charles sent his drive down the middle of the straight par-5 fairway.

Billy followed suit, placing his ball even with Charles' but on the right side near the cart path and a couple lone Maple trees that stood between the 10th and 18th fairway.

As Nicholas began his backswing the sound of a cell phone ringing was heard, causing him to stop his motion and look around. [Another example of distraction is having your cell phone, or any electronic device, sound. Keep equipment in a silent mode or off.]

"Sorry, buddy, I forgot to turn off my ringer," said one of the golfers waiting for their turn to tee off. [Make sure you do not create a disturbance or distraction when someone else it hitting. Cell phones are best left off and in your golf bag.]

"It's ok," said Nicholas, composing himself and refocusing on his shot. His drive sent the ball on a gentle arc, landing in the middle of the fairway, some twenty yards behind the others.

"Nice shot," said Duffy, one of the golfers standing nearby, through slurred speech. [Most courses serve alcohol on the course and in the clubhouse but excess is never stylish. As they say, "drink responsibly".]

"Thanks," Nicholas replied, picking up his tee and heading off.

Nicholas' second shot was unobstructed, but knowing he couldn't reach the green and having no trouble to worry about, played a relaxed hybrid past the ever present holly bushes.

Being a longer hitter, Charles put his second shot on the right side fringe of the green. Billy followed by landing his ball in the center of the fairway, fifty yards from the hole.

Playing a 9-iron, Nicholas dropped his ball on the front edge of the large green.

Charles reached his ball promptly, slightly off Billy's line of play, and began practicing his swing. "You may play, Mr. Roberts. I'm not ready," he said. [If you are on or near someone's line of play you should move. This is respectful so the other player can focus on their shot as well as assure you stay safe.]

At a very comfortable distance, Billy hit a high shot with his lob wedge, the ball coming to rest just a few feet from the flag. "Yee haw," he yelled.

A scowl came across Charles' face for a moment at the loud display, then he went back to his practice swings. [Don't take an excessive amount of time practicing. The USGA recommends 20 seconds for your pre-shot routine.]

After several more rehearsals Charles stepped up to his ball and chipped it to within three feet of the cup.

"Practice makes perfect," he said with a wide grin. Then, walking up to his ball, Charles pulled out the flagstick and, leaning it against his shoulder, tapped his ball in for birdie before replacing the flag. [The rules allow holding the flagstick while putting, as long as doing so isn't done to aid your shot; but with other people on the green still to hit there's no reason not to set the flag down out of everyone's path of play.]

Retrieving his ball, he walked back to his golf cart to clean his putter before putting it away. [Proper etiquette is to wait on the green until everyone has finished holing out before leaving the area. Stay with your group when possible.]

"I'll get it," Billy said through clenched teeth, as he pulled the flagstick from the cup and set it on the ground.

Nicholas rolled his putt but came up a foot short. "Ugh," he said, as he walked up and tapped it in. "I'm happy with par though."

Billy hit his putt but left it short too. A quick reset of his stance and he sank it for par.

RICHARD E. TODD

"**D**ON'T BE FOOLED by this scenic tee box, surrounded by sea oats and having a panoramic view looking down over the course. This short 345 yard par-4 is, in my opinion, the toughest hole on the course," Charles stated. [Providing insight into the layout of a hole to those who haven't played before can be appreciated. Ask your fellow competitors first though, as they may not want your input. And don't come off as a know-it-all.]

"After your drive, which plays down a considerable distance to the fairway, you must negotiate a sharp cut to the right, over a water hazard, to a small green surrounded by tall oak trees. [General comments on the course layout is not considered 'advice' by the USGA and has no associated penalty. Remember to check how much insight to the layout your partners want.] Fear not gentlemen, I shall show you the path," Charles said as he teed and played his drive.

Charles' ball left the tee, heading out towards the fairway that was some thirty yards below the tee box, on a path to the left side fairway, which is lined by trees to separate it from the 15th hole. After a small fade, the ball came to rest in the center of the fairway with a clear shot to the green.

"As I said, follow my lead. You may swing away, Mr. Roberts," Charles stated as he walked off the tee box and down the few wooden steps towards the carts.

Nicholas was standing to the side of the parked carts, practicing his swing. Oblivious to Charles coming near, Nicholas nearly bashed Charles in the head during his backswing. [Always be aware of your surroundings and only practice in a clear area.]

"Mr. Filler, please do take care in swinging your clubs," Charles stated as he ducked out of the way and continued on. [It also should be mentioned that you need to watch where you walk. Take notice of other golfers.]

"Mighty fine shot, Chuck," said Billy as he prepared for his own drive. A flowing swing sent his ball on a mirrored path as Charles', landing five yards further. "But then, mine was better."

Last to play, Nicholas drove his ball down to the fairway, landing on the right side and even with the holly bush marker.

After traveling down the hill, Nicholas came to his lie. He had 150 yards to the protected green. Despite the entire putting surface not being visible due to the tree line and the fairway turning to the right, he decided to go for it. Playing a 7-iron, he swung. The line was good; although, the contact wasn't solid, and the ball came up short, landing in the pond with a large splash.

"Bad luck, old man," Charles stated as he played his second shot. At 95 yards, a pitching wedge was the club of

RICHARD E. TODD

choice, creating a perfect flight and landing on the rear side of the green before taking a hop off the back edge.

"Watch it, Chuck, that bad luck might rub off," Billy stated as he also played a wedge, landing in the center of the green, just a few yards from the cup.

Nicholas stood at the edge of the creek where his ball last crossed the margin of the water hazard, took a few steps back on the line to the flagstick, and dropped a replacement ball. [Knowing the rules of golf and how to properly play from different circumstances shows great etiquette for the game and its noble history. Read 'The Golf Rules' on stroke play golf rules for additional help.] He then easily hit the ball onto the green from this short 50 yard distance.

Charles arrived at his ball first, with Billy and Nicholas still on their way across the bridge. Taking his lob wedge, he began to practice his swing. Standing a tad too close, he clipped the ball, moving it slightly a couple inches to the side. Charles glanced up watchfully to see that his playing partners were still traveling towards the green and unaware of his action. Taking his club, he pulled the ball back to its original spot and took his shot, landing the ball a few feet past the fringe on the green. [The rules require a moved ball to be replaced back to its original spot, sometimes with a penalty. You should inform your playing partners of the events that took place.]

"Looks like we're all ready to dance," Billy stated as he parked the cart before pulling his putter from the golf bag.

Nicholas was furthest out and rolled his putt across the green, just missing the cup to the high side. He then walked to his ball and tapped it in. "That's a bogey for me," he stated.

"I disagree, Mr. Filler," Charles stated. "That's a double-bogey for you. Don't forget your penalty stroke."

"Right. Double. Thanks," Nicholas responded. [Occasionally, someone miscounts their strokes. As long as the error is unintentional there's no harm in politely mentioning the item. There's no need for any slander or insults to get your point across.]

Billy took two strokes to hole his ball for par. "Yea haw," he exclaimed.

Charles' first putt ran a foot past before he sank it. "Bogey for me," he said abruptly. [You are your own referee in the game of golf. Remember to follow all rules and count all strokes, even the ones you didn't mean to make, and don't lie about your strokes. Play fair and take your earned score.]

RICHARD E. TODD

A FTER A SHORT walk to the teeing ground of the par-3 12th hole, two small signs were seen posted: *"Please apply the preferred lie rule in the fairway"* and *"Cart path only this hole"*. [The golf course committee may post special instructions for safety to the golfer or to preserve or maintain the course. Always follow them.]

"What's a preferred lie?" asked Nicholas.

"That's what you northern folk call winter rules. Must be due to the soggy fairway on this hole caused by that storm last night," Billy said. "Simply roll your ball out of any bad lie before you play." [This normally illegal action is occasionally allowed by the course to limit further destruction to the turf because of sensitive or poor playing conditions.]

"Our committee allows you to place your ball within one club-length distance when evoking the preferred lie rule," Charles stated as he started his pre-shot routine. [It is good etiquette to know the local rules when playing.] With only 155 yards to the hole, he played a full 8-iron, landing in the right side bunker. "That's unfortunate," he said aloud.

Billy hit next, placing an 8-iron stroke just on the front of the green, but not before taking a large divot.

"It's playable," he said as he grabbed a scoop of seed mixture from the box sitting next to the tee markers and poured it onto the newly created hole. [If the course provides seed mix, you should use it whenever a divot is taken that can't be replaced, due to the divot being in too many small pieces. This speeds along the healing of the ground and helps keep the course in good condition for future rounds.]

Not being as long a hitter as the others, Nicholas teed off with a 7-iron. He sent his ball on a straight path for the flag. It landed at the front edge of the sloped green, took a hop, and rolled up to within a yard of the cup, leaving a straight, up-hill putt. "Nice," he said.

Leaving the tee box, Charles drove down the cart path, which ran along the left side of the fairway. As he approached the green he turned right and cut across the fairway to the other side of the putting green near the bunker and his ball. [Remember the 'no carts' sign? This is stated to protect the course from excessive damage due to the heavy motorized vehicles on ground that is too wet to support the load. The grounds crew knows where the course needs extra attention and where it is most sensitive and posts signs to signify this. Not following these signs hurts the course and everyone that plays after you.]

Grabbing his sand wedge, Charles entered the hazard from the front side of the bunker, and walked the full length to his ball. [It's best to enter near your ball. This makes the least amount of footprints.] He then took several practice strokes, throwing sand about on the putting green. [Practice strokes are not allowed in bunkers. And throwing sand multiple times on the green is bad etiquette and makes the area more difficult to putt on.] Finally he was ready and chipped his ball out, landing three feet from the hole. Happy with himself, he grabbed the nearest rake and smoothed out his footsteps as he made his way back to his cart. [Always rake bunkers after use. This gives anyone following you the same opportunity for a playable lie.] He threw the rake into the bunker then drove his cart back across the fairway to the cart path. [The locations of rakes is a debatable issue but the USGA recommends placing rakes outside the bunker and parallel to the line of play, preferably along the outer edge of the bunker.]

Billy was first to putt, but Nicholas' ball rested directly on his line.

"Let me mark that for you, Billy," Nicholas stated as he placed a small coin to the side of his ball before picking it up. [Removing your ball when it's in someone's way is considerate, and in some cases required.]

"Thanks, buddy," Billy stated as he rolled his putt up the hill, coming to rest six inches short of the cup. "Well, ain't that all," he said, then walked up, took his stance, and sank his putt for par.

Charles was next and rolled his short putt for par.

Last to play, Nicholas took his stance and stroked the ball. Despite his short putt, the ball stopped a foot from the hole. He then left his second putt short an inch. "Rats," he said, half smiling, as he tapped it in for a bogey.

[Golf is a difficult game, measured in inches. Don't let your performance dictate your mood.]

RICHARD E. TODD

A S BILLY, CHARLES, and Nicholas walked off the green of the 12th hole they spotted a small, nearby concession stand, surrounded by golfers, that was selling drinks and snacks. This shed was the hub for several holes. The 12th green, the 13th tee, the 14th green, and the 15th tee box all bordered this building. As they came closer to the stand, the noise from this crowd grew louder.

The group on the 15th tee had a radio with them that was playing loud jazz music. [Loud music, or noise of any sorts, is a distraction to other golfers. Keep it down.]. The group ahead of Charles' group, teeing off on the 13th hole, were shouting profane words at each other's drives. [Profanity doesn't belong on the course. Be a gentlemen at all times.] Another group was having a heated discussion whether or not to hit balls at the group ahead of them in an effort to motivate that group to play faster. [Never hit golf balls at other players. It's dangerous and very bad-mannered.]

"Maybe we should just call the fairway police," one golfer said. [If you have any trouble on the course, contact a course ranger or the clubhouse.]

One group waiting to tee off was heard talking about the banking business. [Be cautious when talking about work on the golf course. Not everyone is willing to let the outside world onto the golf course and into their game.]

The time came for Charles to tee off. During his backswing he was startled by the sound of a golf cart skidding across gravel. [Take care in operating a golf cart, for the sake of the course, for your safety, the cart itself, and for the consideration of other golfers.]

"Riffraff," he mumbled as he regained his composure and started his swing over, sending his ball down the left side of the fairly straight 13th fairway, landing past the holly bush marker on the par-4 hole.

As had become the norm, Billy played next. He hit a screamer down the center of the fairway. Getting a nice kick, it rolled ten yards past Charles' ball. With a smile, he stepped back for Nicholas to take his turn.

It was noticed, after a short but awkward moment, Nicholas wasn't with them. A quick scan around the area found Nicholas waiting to use the nearby ball washer. The player in front of him seemed to be washing an entire bag of some questionable golf balls. [Don't overdo it. You only need to wash a ball or two at a time, especially if others are waiting to use the equipment.]

Seeing his group waiting for him, Nicholas sacrificed a clean ball and ran back to the teeing ground for his shot, which he landed down the fairway on the right side, just short of the holly.

At his ball, Nicholas waited for the group ahead of them

to putt out before taking his next stroke. As he watched, he noticed one of the players had set his golf bag near the edge of the green. [Be careful where you place equipment when near the green. It doesn't take much to damage the turf.]

As the group started to clear off the green, Nicholas began his pre-shot routine. [Be ready to hit when it's clear and your turn. Don't hold up others while you prepare.] He then played a 7-iron to the front of the green.

Charles chipped onto the center of the green, as did Billy.

Without much fanfare, each player two putt for par.

RICHARD E. TODD

O N THE 14TH tee box, Charles prepared for his drive. There wasn't any trouble to contend with on this par-4 as the hole played straight, but long, to a slightly elevated green with bunkers on the left and the right sides. The left side of the fairway bordered the edge of the course, and the out of bounds was protected by a dense row of trees, while the right side had only a few sparsely-planted young trees that separated it from the oncoming 13th hole. A big swing sent his ball down the center of the fairway.

Billy played next, landing his drive even with Charles' ball but closer to the right side rough.

As Nicholas prepared for his drive a grounds keeper was seen driving down the out of bounds side of the fairway. Nicholas took a step back to wait for him to pass.

"Feel free to swing away, Mr. Filler," Charles said. "If any of those maintenance workers are on the course during an outing they deserve anything that happens to them." [Remember, it's the grounds crew's job to constantly provide upkeep to the course. It's to their credit that you can play a well-manicured course. If they are working, give them a moment to finish and clear out of your way. It's safe and courteous.]

In less than a minute the cart was out of range, and the driver waved in gratitude as he drove away.

Nicholas then played. He had a solid drive, landing on the right side of the fairway but much shorter than the others.

Still up to hit, Nicholas played his second shot from just outside two hundred yards. His hybrid made solid contact, sending the ball on a direct path for the right side bunker.

"Get left, get left," Billy yelled. [No one likes it when someone else yells at your ball to do something that physics won't permit. Yell at your own ball. Or, better yet, don't yell at any ball.]

Not paying any attention to the directive, the ball landed in the center of the bunker.

Billy, 165 yards out, played a 7-iron to the front of the green.

Charles landed his shot short of the green in the left side bunker. "Rats. I didn't get that club quite square." [Don't state the obvious or make excuses as if you are a PGA instructor and know what you did. Accept the shot wasn't as intended and move to the next stroke. Golf is not a game of perfect, even for professionals.]

Nicholas reached the bunker first. His ball was sitting nicely up on the sand. He stepped into the bunker and took his stance to play his shot. As he started his backswing he saw sand fly up into the air from the other side of the green, then Charles' ball landed with a thud near the flagstick. [Be sure it's your turn to hit and that no one else is swinging at the same time. This can cause a distraction, and your ball could possible hit another player.]

Once Charles' ball came to a stop, Nicholas set himself again and swung. [Don't hit while another ball is in motion. It's hard for others to help track multiple balls at the same time and, in some cases, it's against the rules.] His ball flew high and landed on the green, inside of Charles'. As he walked out of the bunker he noticed an empty bottle on the ground. [It's unlikely this bottle has been lying so close to the green all day, so another golfer must have left it. Do your part to keep the course clear of your garbage. You can also clean up after others.] Picking up the bottle, Nicholas walked it back to a nearby garbage can, then headed to his ball.

Billy had a straight, fifteen foot uphill putt from the front of the green. A strong stroke sent it on a path for the hole, but the ball stopped a few inches away. "Dangnabit," he said, then walked up to the ball and stroked it in into the cup.

Charles hit next. Leaving his putt a foot short.

"That's good enough for me, Chuck," Billy said, hitting the ball back to Charles. [Don't hit another person's ball. Allow them the opportunity to hole it out and hear that lovely sound as the ball rattles around inside the cup. Plus, it's against the rules.]

Nicholas lined up his putt and stroked the ball, leaving it on the lip of the cup.

A loud groan, along with some laughing, was heard from other golfers nearby that were watching while waiting in line at the snack shack. [It's nice to show support for others, but let's keep the negative noises and comments to yourself.] Nicholas glanced up, then walked over and tapped his ball in.

RICHARD E. TODD

15

Chapter

STILL IN THE crowded hub of these four holes and wanting something to drink, Nicholas stood in line again at the concession stand. [If you are getting drinks or snacks for yourself, see if others in your group want something, too. That way the group stays together, and no one feels left out.]

"What can I get you?" the attendant asked the person standing in front of Nicholas.

"Two iced teas," he replied.

"How's your round going?" she asked, making small talk as she poured the drinks.

"I'm doing okay, but I normally play much better. A lot better. I guess I'm having an off day." [Don't talk about how good you normally play. The past is the past, and no one cares.]

"Sorry about that. Here's your drinks. Enjoy the rest of your round."

"Thanks, Christine," he said after reading her nametag.

"And what can I get you?" she asked Nicholas.

Upon receiving his order, Nicholas paid his bill, left a

tip, and headed back to his group, who were now at the next tee box. [Tipping isn't always required, but many workers do rely on gratuities to supplement their income.]

Charles planted a tee, set his ball, and stroked a 5-wood out to the middle of the fairway, near the holly, where the par-4 hole took a turn to the left. His ball coming to rest ten yards from the woods that bordered the right edge of this hole.

"Hey, this guy just scored 15 on the last hole," another golfer yelled from the previous hole, pointing to a rather embarrassed and intoxicated individual. [While the rules require you to play every hole and hit until you hole out, in non-competition golf you can pick up your ball and forego finishing the hole. This option should be considered when your strokes exceed the USGA's 'ESC' score (Equitable Stroke Control), or double the par for that hole. This helps keep up the speed of the game and doesn't increase the wait time for all the golfers playing behind you on the course.]

After a short laugh, Billy played next, sending his drive along the same path but landing a few yards shorter, leaving himself an open shot to the green.

"Make sure you keep your drive to the right, away from them trees. They were planted to block anyone from trying to cut the dogleg on this hole," Billy said as he stepped off the teeing ground." [Keep advice to yourself. Let everyone play their own game. It's disrespectful and against the rules.]

As Nicholas bent down to tee up his ball he noticed the end of a cigar on the ground, which he picked up and tossed near the trash can. [Always clean up after yourself, and sometimes after others. Trash cans are frequently available on the course.] A little waggle and he sent his drive to the far right side of the fairway.

"Well, you kept it away from the trees. Sorry about the extra twenty yards you now have to the hole," Billy said.

Heading over to his ball, Nicholas exited the cart and prepared to play his shot. Taking a second glance down at the ground he realized this wasn't his ball. It wasn't even a ball, it was a large marshmallow. Looking around, he noticed several of them lying about.

These must have been dropped on the course by some practical joker trying to fool some unsuspecting golfers, Nicholas thought. *And I fell for it.* [The concept of the joke is funny, but it delays play for everyone on the course and makes additional work for grounds keepers.]

Seeing his actual ball nearby, Nicholas addressed and stroked it with his 7-iron, landing the ball just short of the front of the inclined green, just missing the bunker that was on the right side.

Billy played next and dropped his ball onto the green, just left of Nicholas'.

Charles followed suit, landing on the front of the green but a yard closer to the flagstick.

As the group proceeded to the green a loud pop was heard from the tee box, like that from a firecracker. Looking back they saw the group that was playing behind them chuckling and wobbling around with laughter as one of the players picked up a wooden match that had been hit against the ball just struck. This caused the loud sound due to the compression of the match between the driver and the ball. [Have fun when playing golf but do so in a manner that increases the respect of the game.]

Being just off the fringe and having a twenty foot up-hill putt, Nicholas played his 7-iron again, running the ball up to the hole and past it a couple feet.

Charles then took his stance and stroked his ball to within a foot of the cup.

"Nice putt, slim, but next time watch where you're standing," Billy stated while pointing to his ball and Charles' feet, which were both directly on his line of play. [Do not stand on another player's intended putting line. Spike marks from shoes can create irregularities in the grass which can cause the ball to roll off-line.]

"Sorry old man," Charles said as he walked towards the cup.

Shaking his head, Billy hit his ball up the hill. "Get legs" he yelled, as the ball slowed down and came to rest a few inches short of the hole. [Telling an inanimate object to behave a certain way is crazy and nonproductive. Try to do it quietly if you must at all. Most golfers do this, so maybe we're all a little crazy.]

"Tarnation," he said as he walked up to his ball and tapped it in for par.

Nicholas was away and stroked his putt, but it stopped on the edge of the hole. "Drop," he said as he jumped up and down once in an attempt to knock it in by shaking the ground. [The golf ball should only be moved by strokes made with clubs and nothing else. Jumping to make the earth move is illegal.] Not falling, he walked up and tapped in for bogey.

Calmly, Charles rolled his putt in for par.

"AND HERE WE are, gentlemen. The toughest ranked hole on the course," Charles said, referring to the 350 yard, par-4, 16th hole. [This information is public knowledge, as it's listed on the scorecard. Stating this is not considered advice, but rather small talk, and is allowed by the rules and is acceptable conversation.]

Charles took the lead, playing a 4-wood down the fairway. His ball coming to rest a few yards from the 150 yard marker, adjacent to the holly bush, leaving him a perfect shot to the green, which was 90 degrees to the left and at the top of a hill. "Perfect," he said.

Billy also hit a gentle shot, aiming for the center of the fairway. "Uh oh. I got all of that one," he said having finished his swing, watching the ball flying further than he wanted. It first landed near the holly bush then took a big bounce and rolled slightly past the dogleg, towards a small pond that separated the 16th and the 2nd hole. "I should be ok," he said to himself, walking off the tee box.

Nicholas played a 5-wood for his drive. His tee shot

headed towards the right side of the fairway, near a few sparse trees that divided the 16th and the 3rd hole.

"Get left, get left," Billy yelled as the ball landed and rolled into the first cut of rough. [Yelling at someone else's ball just points out their mistake and is insensitive. Mind your own game and leave others' to theirs.] "Sorry, partner," Bill continued as Nicholas' ball settled off the fairway.

Still away, Nicholas played a 3-wood towards the hole. His shot didn't have enough distance nor height and landed on the hillside, twenty yards short of the green.

As Billy came near his lie, he caught sight of a golfer walking around the pond, carrying a small bag and collecting abandoned golf balls. By the looks of the bag he had at least two dozen golf balls. [Hunting for balls isn't illegal but isn't highly respected. Also know that many of the balls found are unplayable due to the length of time they are left in poor conditions. If you do search, just make sure to not hold up play while you 'shop' for your next sleeve of balls.]

"I think I saved myself fifty dollars," the golfer yelled to Billy, holding up his collection and continuing his shopping spree.

As Billy prepared to play, he called over to Charles. "Where's the flag?" [You can ask for help in certain situations. Asking for positions of public items is one example that's permitted.]

"I can't locate it from here," Charles stated. "It must be at the back of the green." [If asked for help and you can legally provide it, do so honestly and as accurately as possible.]

"Ok," said Billy, as he played a 7-iron and sent his ball up and onto the green. "Good call. Thanks," he yelled back.

[Remember your manners, always use please and thank you.]

Charles, with a perfect line, pitched his ball to the putting green, too.

Finding his ball in a fairly good lie, Nicholas chipped it onto the green with a well-played sand wedge.

Coming upon the green, the flagstick was found on the ground. [Make sure you leave any area in the same, or better, condition than you originally found it.]

"Looks like the group ahead forgot to replace the flag," Billy stated. "Is it in anyone's way?" he asked. [It's always polite to check if anyone needs equipment or people moved so they can make their stroke without restrictions.]

Hearing none, he lined up his putt and made his stroke, the ball stopping two feet short of the hole. A quick audible sigh, and Billy was lining up his putt again. This time he missed it high before taking his third putt and holing it, earning bogey.

Charles, on his walk across the green to his ball, bent down and placed a marker by Nicholas' ball, before picking it up, and handing the ball to him. "Your ball was on my putting path," he said as he continued to his own ball. [You should ask permission before marking or touching another person's ball.]

Charles, with fifteen feet, stroked his ball a yard past the hole, then left it short a few inches when trying to run it back, before sinking it in the hole for bogey.

Replacing his ball, Nicholas played. He left his putt short a foot, then taking a second stroke, he holed out for bogey.

"Tough hole," Nicholas said as the group headed to the next tee box.

RICHARD E. TODD

ON THE 17ᵀᴴ hole, an 8-iron sent Charles' ball 155 yards, over a shallow grass-filled ravine, onto the green of this par-3. "Brilliant," he said to himself, stepping off the teeing ground.

Billy teed his ball and stroked his tee shot to the back-right side of the green. "Yee-haw," he said. "This rodeo is coming to a close on a high note."

Nicholas' swing produced a hook and sent the ball to the left side of the fairway and twenty yards short of the green.

Mounting their cart, Billy drove Nicholas to his ball. After Nicholas exited and pulled out a wedge and his putter, Billy drove to the other side of the green and parked near his own ball and the next tee box. [Optimally, park carts between the putting green you are on and the next hole, this helps to increase pace of play so the golfers behind you don't have to wait excessively to hit while you leave the green.]

Nicholas prepared for his chip onto the green. After a few practice swings, he felt he needed a more lofted club but, seeing golfers starting to gather back on the tee box, chose to use the club he had rather than hold up play by running across the fairway to his golf bag then back to his lie. [Playing ready golf is the goal, and sometimes that means hitting in less than optimal circumstances. A creative golfer can use the same club for different type shots.] Simply playing the ball slightly forward in his stance gave him the extra loft he wanted, and Nicholas was able to land his ball on the green, pin high and left.

As Nicholas headed to the green, he saw another group on the adjacent hole driving down the fairway. They had crammed three people in the cart, with one of the players dragging his golf bag off the side of the cart as there wasn't room in the bag spaces. [There's a reason you only generally find two straps on the back of a golf cart – because only two bags, and two people, should be carried. Overweighting a golf cart can be hazardous for the vehicle. And dragging equipment down the fairway can damage the turf for all players.]

"After you, Chuck," Billy said.

"I believe you are away," Charles responded after a visual inspection.

"Looks like we're both about the same distance. You wanna go?" he asked.

"I prefer more time to prepare my shot. You may play," Charles said. [When in doubt to distance and who should play next, simply go with ready golf rules, and whomever is prepared should play next to keep the pace going.]

"Fine by me," Billy said as he stroked his putt down the slight incline towards the hole, his ball coming to rest a few

RICHARD E. TODD

inches past the cup. A quick tap and he holed out for par.

By now, Charles was ready and sent his ball on a path for the hole which stopped an inch to the side of the hole. A flip of the putter and his ball rolled to the bottom of the cup. "Bully," he said.

With a short third shot, Nicholas, too, finished with a par.

"Let me see. That is par for me, Mr. Roberts, and Mr. Filler," Charles said as he pulled out the score card and pencil and began marking down the scores. [You should not tally scores on the green, this delays hitting by those playing behind you. Mark down your scores either on the next tee box or at least off the green.]

"One last hole, gentlemen."

RICHARD E. TODD

18
Chapter

"READY TO TAKE 'er home," Billy asked as Charles teed up for the par-4 last hole.

Despite its straight fairway and nominal trouble, the length at 475 yards from tee to pin made up for it.

Charles let loose his best drive of the day. A gentle fade landed his ball just outside the two hundred yard marker.

Before picking up his tee, Charles gave a gentle wave to the club members sitting on the veranda of the clubhouse, as they watched everyone play the closing hole.

Billy teed and swung, landing his drive just behind Charles.

Nicholas, hoping to keep up with the rest of his group, practiced with as much power in his swing as he could muster. [Although not an etiquette item, remember to play your game. A fluid swing is better than a forced one.]

Stepping up to the ball, he let it rip. The ball started down the middle then took off for the right side, on a path for the golfers on the adjacent fairway.

"That's heading at that group," Billy said quickly to

Nicholas in a worried tone. "You gonna yell fore?"

[The word 'fore' is used to alert others of the impending danger of being hit by an errant shot. There's no harm in calling this when the impact is uncertain as it's better to alert others and have the ball miss everyone than not yell it and have someone struck.]

Nicholas just stood there watching the ball flight as it headed closer to the unsuspecting players.

"Fore on the right," yelled Billy. [Anyone can yell fore, it doesn't have to be the player who hit the ball. Help out others when they are unsure or unwilling to call this out, you could save a life.]

Immediately, the group coming up the fairway took cover behind their golf carts as the ball landed just several feet away from them and rolled past and into their fairway. One of them gave a quick wave of thanks at the warning as they continued play.

"Close one, partner. Let's go get that back on the right hole," Billy said as he and Nicholas climbed into their cart and headed out.

At the area where the two fairways touched, Billy parked the cart. Nicholas looked up the oncoming fairway to assure no one was hitting, then quickly darted out to his ball. [When your ball is in another fairway you need to let those playing the hole have priority over your shot. And make sure the area is safe to enter.] A short waggle and a swing with his 3-wood sent the ball back onto the correct hole and towards the green, coming to rest in the fairway, on the right side.

Still two hundred yards out, Billy stroked his hybrid. His

ball landed in the fairway then rolled onto the front of the green.

"I'm on the dance floor," Billy said.

Charles, too, hit a perfectly played shot, landing on the front of the putting green and, rolling up the slope, stopped pin high. Faint cheers were heard from the clubhouse, and a smile crossed Charles' face.

With his pitching wedge, Nicholas hit his ball onto the green, six feet right of the hole.

With everyone on, Charles pulled the flagstick from the cup and gently put it down to the back side of the green, out of the path of all putting lines.

Billy and Nicholas looked at each other with puzzled expressions, as this was the first time Charles had helped out all day. [Its proper etiquette to share in the upkeep and work of the group. Take your turn tending the flag, tracking shots, buying snacks or drinks, driving, and giving compliments.] Realizing it was a show for the other members that were watching, they returned to their game.

Billy rolled his putt up the green towards the hole, coming to rest a foot short. A groan was heard from the ever growing crowd. [In a friendly, non-professional round of golf, keep your negative comments to yourself to avoid compounding the ill feelings the player might have after a shot didn't go the way they wanted.]

"Rascal," Billy said as he walked up to his ball and tapped it in.

Nicholas played next, and rolled his ball in for par.

Charles, taking his time to line up his putt, dropped his ball in for birdie to the cheers of those watching.

"Good game gentlemen," Charles said, extending his arm to shake hands with each of his competitors.

"Yup, good game there slim. You're a tough one," Billy said, shaking Charles' hand. [It's always polite to shake each players hand after a round of golf.]

"And you did just fine for not playing here before, Nicholas," Billy said, now shaking Nicholas' hand.

"Well done, Mr. Filler," Charles said, taking his turn to shake with him.

"Did I hear something about some grub after the round," Billy asked.

"Yes, we are providing a meal and additional refreshments," Charles responded.

"May I take your clubs, Mr. Hound?" asked one of the attendants who promptly appeared and grabbed Charles' golf bag. [At some resorts and courses your clubs may be cleaned after your round by staff. This is a special service, and you should tip the person who cleans your clubs, if appropriate.]

"Of course," said Charles as he walked off the green.

"And you, sirs?" another attendant asked Billy and Nicholas.

"You bet," Billy replied.

"Sure," Nicholas said. [If you are a guest at a club and unsure how to proceed, just follow the lead of your host.]

"Let's retire to the veranda, and we shall see who came in second," Charles said with a grin, walking towards the clubhouse.

RICHARD E. TODD

THE GROUP WAS seated together at a round table, set with fine china and exquisite cutlery. This was definitely not the normal post-round eating environment Nicholas was used to at his local municipal course. Where were the plastic forks and condiments in colored plastic squeeze containers? Even the tablecloth, which was a stark white, could be seen to be of very high quality.

"I've tallied the scores for our round. Did we say we would wager by skins, Nassau, or a combination?" Charles asked. [All betting should be agreed to before the round starts. The USGA also states that wagers should not be excessive in nature.]

"We're just out for a fun round, slick. So tell us how we ended," Billy said.

At that moment the buzz of a microphone was heard, followed by an announcement.

"Good evening, everyone. I'm Richard Todd, chairman of the board for Fox Hunters Country Club. I'd like to thank all who attended and helped run this year's annual community fund raiser. The efforts allowed us to donate $50,000 to the local shelter. They provide food for the hungry, a bed for the homeless, and a friend for the lonely. I hope you enjoyed your round today, and if not, you can at least enjoy this meal," he said, followed by enthusiastic applause. "And as we celebrate helping others, we here at Fox Hunters Country Club would like to give our annual award to the golfer that portrayed these same characteristics today, showing care for the course, good sportsmanship, assisting others, and general friendliness to competitors. This year's recipient is Nicholas Filler."

"Ain't that something special. Congrats," Billy said over the applause from the room, slapping a hand on Nicholas' back.

"Thanks again, and we hope to see everyone next year," Richard said.

As the applause subsided and the indistinct roar of many conversations began, Charles continued his presentation of the scores.

"As I was saying. Mr. Filler posted an 82, Mr. Roberts earned a 72, and I had the lowest score at 71. [When comparing scores it's helpful to use the USGA handicap system to make the round equitable, enjoyable, and a fair competition, regardless of golfing ability.] Don't fret. It's not just my great golfing ability that allowed me to win, there's the home course advantage and all. [Be a gracious winner, or you might have very few people willing to golf with you.]

"You won fair and square, Chuck. Congratulations," replied Billy.

"Good game," Nicholas said. [And be a gracious loser.

Even the greatest of players have off days.]

"Too bad we didn't wager. You could have paid for my club dues," Charles stated. [If you do bet, pay up right away after the round is scored.]

As the meal finished, a sharply dressed individual approached the table.

"Mr. Todd," Charles spoke and immediately stood.

"Hello Charles," he replied. "Sit, please."

"Mr. Filler. I hope you enjoyed our little links."

"Definitely. It's a beautiful course," Nicholas said.

"Thank you. Our grounds crew does an exceptional job. I'm glad you were able to be part of this event."

"Me too. It's a very good cause," replied Nicholas.

"Mr. Roberts, I presume," said Mr. Todd to Billy.

"All my life," Billy responded.

"I heard you played a rather good game today."

"Fair. I've only played the course once before, so I'm still learning it."

"How would you like to change that? That is, if you are still interested in membership here at Fox Hunters Country Club."

"I sure am, but I thought you didn't have any current openings."

"We should be having one opening very soon," Mr. Todd said as he stared at Charles with a very disapproving look. "Our membership committee should be in touch with you soon, Mr. Roberts. Good night everyone."

"Oh, and Charles. Can you stop by the office tomorrow? I would like to discuss your round today in further detail."

"Of course," Charles said with a gulp.

RICHARD E. TODD

CHAPTER 20

CONCLUSION

"WELCOME HOME, YOU country club golfer," Hannah said as Nicholas walked in the door. "How did it go?"

"Great! I learned a lot from that book, *The Golf Rules-Etiquette*, which I was able to apply to my round. And seeing how some people break the rules and have such disregard for sportsmanship and manners, it makes me want to buy everyone a copy. I played very well and had a memorable time. I can't wait to go back. I might have a friend who will be a member soon."

RICHARD E. TODD

THE GOLF RULES—ETIQUETTE

Are you interested in learning about the rules of golf or just want to enjoy another round with this group? Pick up a copy of the book that started it all, *The Golf Rules*, focusing on stroke play format.

Also available, *Short Stories for the Long Links*, a collection of humorous short stories about golf. Visit TheGolfRules.com for information.

And watch for the next release in the *The Golf Rules* book series on match play.

Follow TGR on Facebook, Twitter, WordPress, YouTube, and on our website.

www.**TheGolfRules**.com

Made in the USA
Columbia, SC
05 July 2022

62805479R00067